MW00343651

POEMS and PROSE POEMS
with "The book, spiritual instrument" and
"A throw of the dice…"

by STÉPHANE MALLARMÉ

FENNVILLE, MICHIGAN
2016

Translations copyright 2008-2015 by Jim Hanson

Jim Hanson
2907 63rd Street
Fennville MI 49408
http://jimhanson.org

Contents

POEMS

POEMS

Salute

Nothing, this foam, virgin verse
Not to characterize the cup
So far many a one of a troupe
Of sirens drown themselves upside down

We navigate, oh my various
Friends, me there on the stern
You on the lavish bow which cuts
The flood of lightnings and of winters

A beautiful drunkenness engages me
Without even being afraid of its reeling
To bear this salute upright

Solitude, reef, star
In every respect earned
The white concern of our canvas

The Jinx

Above the dazed cattle of the human beings
The wild manes of the beggars of blue
Bounced their feet in the light on our paths

A black wind on their march spread for banners
Flogging it from cold even in the flesh
As it also ploughed there out of irritable ruts

Always with the hope of meeting the sea
They traveled without bread, without sticks, and without urns
Biting into the golden lemon of the bitter ideal

Most of them grumbled in the night parades
Getting drunk on the happiness of seeing blood flow
Oh Death, the only kiss on their taciturn mouths!

Their defeat, it is by a very powerful angel
Standing on the horizon with its naked steel
A crimson cold in the grateful breast

They suck the pain as they sucked the dream
And when they go giving rhythm to sensual tears
The people kneel down and their mother gets up

They are consoled, safe and majestic
But drag in their steps a hundred brothers at whom we scoff
Derisory martyrs of tortuous chance

The same salt of tears eats away their sweet cheek
They eat the ashes with the same love
But fate is vulgar or comic as it turns

They could incite so like a drum
The slavish pity of races with dull voices
Equal to Prometheus whom a vulture overlooks

No, vile and frequenting deserts with no water
They roam under the whip of a furious monarch
The Jinx, whose incredible laughter prostrates them

Lovers, he jumped in behind to three, willing to share
Then the enduring torrent plunges you in a puddle
And leaves a muddy block of the white swimming couple

Thanks to him, if the one blows its bizarre trombone
From children who will twist us into stubborn laughter
Who, with a fist in their ass, will mimic the brass band

Thanks to him, if the one adorns a faded breast just in time
With a rose who rekindles him ready to marry
With the slobber gleaming on its damned bouquet

And this dwarfish skeleton, wearing a feather
And kicked, the armpit of which has for true hairs of verses
For them is the infinity of the vast bitterness

Upset, they are not going to provoke the pervert
Their creaking rapier follows the moonbeam
Which snows on his carcass and which passes through

Saddened without the pride which crowns misfortune
And sad to avenge the bones of knocks of beak
They covet hatred, instead of resentment

They are the fun of the wipers of viols
Of the kids, the whores and the old trash
Of the tatters dancing when the pitcher is dry

The poets good for alms or revenge
Know the evil of these erased gods
They call them boring and without intelligence

They can run away having enough of each exploit
Like a virgin horse, foams of storms
Rather than to leave in an armored gallop

We shall get drunk on incense the conqueror of the feast
But them, why not put on these wandering players
In scarlet rags yelling that one stops!

When facing them spat out scorn
Useless and the beard with low words asking the thunder
These heroes were exasperated by playful weaknesses

They're going to hang themselves from the streetlamps like figures of fun

Apparition

The moon turned sad. Of seraphim in tears
Dreaming, the bow in the fingers, in the calm
Of transparent flowers, shooting of dying viols
Of white tears rolling on the blue of corollas.
—It was the blessed day of your first kiss.
My affectionate reverie tormented me.
It cleverly intoxicated me with the scent of sadness
That even without regret or lingering disappointment
The gathering of a Dream to the heart that has gathered it.
I wandered there, my eye glued to the old pavement
When the sun on your hair, in the street
And in the evening, you appeared to me with a laugh
And I thought to see the fairy with hat of light
Who once passed by my sweet spoiled child's sleep
Always letting his badly clenched fists
Sprinkle white bouquets of fragrant stars.

Useless Request

Princess! Being (as you are) jealous of the fate of Hebe
Who dawned over this cup in the kiss of your lips
I wear out my fires but discreetly I have only the rank of abbot
And I shall not even be shown naked on Sèvres.

As I am not your bearded lapdog
Neither the bullet nor the crimson, nor the precious games
And what about me? I know your closed downcast glance
Blonde whose divine hairdressers are goldsmiths!

Name us. . .you of whom so many raspberry laughs
Turn us into a herd of tamed lambs
To all grazing the wishes and bleating in the frenzies

Name us. . so that the winged Love of a fan
Combs me there, a flute in my fingers, putting this fold to sleep
Princess, name us a shepherd of your smiles

The Clown Punished

Eyes, lakes with my simple drunkenness reborn
Other than the troubadour who evoked the gesture
As with a quill, of oil lamps' ignoble smoke
I pierced a window in the linen wall

From my leg and arms clear treacherous swimmer
In increasing leaps and bounds, denying the bad
Hamlet! It's as if in the wave I invented
A thousand sepulchers for it, virgin, to disappear

Hilarious gold of a cymbal with angry fists
Suddenly the sun strikes the nudity
That exhaled my pure freshness of mother-of-pearl

When you passed over me, stale night of the skin
Not knowing, ingrate! that it was all my consecration
This rouge drowned in the water of faithless glaciers

A Black Woman…

A black woman shaken by the demon
Wants to taste of a sad infant, a new and
Criminal fruit under their torn clothes
This glutton gets ready for crafty work

To her belly she happily compares two nipples
And, so high that the hand will not know how to capture
She shoots the dark shock of her boots
Like some inept tongue unrestrainedly

Against the fearful nudity of a gazelle
Who trembles, on her back like a mad elephant
Reversed she waits and admires herself with zeal,
Laughing with her naïve teeth at the child;

And on her legs where the victim is laid down,
Lifting a black skin opened under the hair
Ahead of this strange mouth's palate
Pale and pink as a marine shellfish

The Windows

Tired of the sad hospital and of the foul incense
That rises against the commonplace whiteness of the curtains
Toward the huge crucifix bored by the empty wall
There the sly dying man straightens his old back,

Drags himself and goes, less to warm his decay
Than to see the sun on the stones, to paste
The white hairs and the bones of a meager figure
On the windows that a lovely clear beam wants to tan

And his mouth, feverish and of voracious blue azure
That young one, he went to inhale his treasure
A virginal skin and from the past. To soil
From a long bitter kiss the warm golden stone floors.

Drunk, he lives, forgetting the horror of holy oils,
The herb teas, the clock, and the imposed bed,
The cough, and when the evening bleeds among the tiles,
His eye, on the light-drenched horizon

Sees golden galleys, beautiful as swans
On a river of purple and perfumes sleeping
In rocking the wild lightning and rich in their lines
In a great indifference loaded with memory!

Thus, taken by disgust of the man with the harsh soul
Sprawled on happiness, where his only appetites
Eat, and who persists in searching this refuse
To offer the woman suckling her children,

I flee and I cling to all the windows
From which one turns a shoulder to life and, blessed,
In their glass, washed of eternal dew,
That gilds the chaste mornings of Infinity

I see myself and find I am an angel! And I die, and I love
—Whether the window is art, or mysticism—
To come back to life, carrying my dream in a crown
In the previous sky where Beauty flowered!

But alas, here below is the master: dread of it
Sometimes makes me lose heart, until this safe haven
And the impure vomiting of Stupidity
Forces me to hold my nose in front of the azure

Is there a way, oh Self who knows bitterness
To push the crystal by the offended monster
And run away from me, with my two featherless wings
—At the risk of falling throughout eternity?

The *Flowers*

From the golden avalanches of the old blue
On the first day and from the eternal snow of stars
Once you undid the big calyxes for
The land still young and innocent of disasters

The wild gladiolus, with the slender necked swans
And that divine laurel of exiled souls
Crimson as the pure toe of a seraph
Which reddens the modesty of strident dawns

The hyacinth, the myrtle with its adorable flash
And, like the flesh of a woman, the cruel
Rose, Herodias in flower in the bright garden
The one that a fierce and dazzling blood sprays!

And you made the sobbing whiteness of lilies
Whoever rolling on seas of sighs they touch
Through blue incense from the paler horizons
Rising dreamily toward the moon that weeps!

Hosanna on the cittern and the censers
Our Lady, hosanna from the garden of our limbo,
And eventually echoed by the heavenly evenings
Ecstasy of the glances, sparkling of the halos

Oh Mother who created in your righteous and broad breast
A calyx rocking the future flask
Of big flowers with soothing Death
For the tired poet who life wilts

Revival

The sickly spring sadly chased away
The winter, the season of serene art, the lucid winter,
And, in my being in whom the glum blood presides
Impotence stretches itself in a long yawn

White twilights warm under my skull
Which an iron circle squeezes thus which an old grave
And sad, I roam after a vague and lovely dream,
By the fields where the immense sap struts about

Then I fall irritated by the scent of trees, tired,
And digging a pit with my face in my dream,
Biting the warm ground where lilacs grow,

I wait, by damaging me my boredom rises…
—However the Azure laughs on the hedge and the awakening
Of so many birds in flower chirping in the sun.

Anxiety

I do not come tonight to possess your body, oh beast
To whom go the sins of a people, nor to dig
In your impure hair a sad storm
Under an incurable boredom that sheds my kiss:

I ask your bed for the heavy sleep without dreams
Smoothing under the unknown curtains of remorse
And that you can taste after your black lies
You who know more about the void than the dead do

For Vice, gnawing my native nobility,
Has marked me, like you, with its infertility
But since your stony breast is inhabited

By a heart which the tooth of crime does not hurt
I run away, pale, undone, haunted by my shroud
Being afraid to die when I sleep alone

"Tired of bitter rest"

Tired of bitter rest where my laziness offends
A glory for which I once fled the adorable
Childhood of rosewood under the natural
Blue, and seven times more tired of a harsh pact
To dig by evening a new pit
In the avaricious and cold ground of my brain,
Gravedigger without pity for infertility,
—What shall I say to this Dawn, oh Dreams, visited
By the roses, when for fear of its pallid roses,
The vast cemetery unites the empty holes?—
I want to abandon the voracious Art of a cruel
Country, and, smiling at old reproaches
Which my friends make to me, the past, the genius,
And my lamp that however knows my agony
Imitating the Chinese with a clear and fine heart
To whom pure ecstasy is to paint the end
On his cups of snow to the delighted moon
From a bizarre flower that perfumes his transparent
Life, the flower which he smelled, child,
Being grafted onto the blue filigree of a soul.
And death as the only dream of a wise man,
Serenely, I am going to choose a young landscape
That I would paint again on a cup, distracted,
A line of thin and pale blue would be
A lake, amid the sky of bare china,
A clear crescent lost in a white cloud
Dips its calm horn in the icy waters
Not far from three big emerald eyelashes, the reeds

The Bell Ringer

While the bell that awakens, its voice clear
In clean air and translucent and deep in the morning
And passes on the child who throws an angelus
To please it amongst the lavender and thyme

The bell ringer touched by the bird he enlightens
Riding sadly by groaning in Latin
On the stone which stretches the age-old rope
Intending to lower to him only a distant ringing

I am that man. Alas! From the willing night
I may pull the cord to ring out the Ideal,
From cold sins a feudal plumage cavorts

And the voice comes only to me through scraps, hollow
—But one day, tired of pulling with no result
Oh Satan, I shall remove the stone and hang myself.

Summer Sadness

The sun on the sand, oh sleeping wrestler
Warms a languorous bath in the gold of your hair
And burning the incense on your enemy cheek
It blends an amorous drink with your tears

Of this white blaze, the immutable lull
Made you say, saddened, oh my fearful kisses
"We shall never be a mummy, alone
Under the ancient desert and the fortunate palms"

But your hair is a tepid river
Where the soul that obsesses us drowns without a shiver
And to find that Void that you do not know

I will taste the mascara your eyelids wept
To see if it can give the heart you struck
The senselessness of the sky and of the stones

The Blue

From the eternal blue the serene irony
Devastates, indolently lovely like the flowers
Across a barren desert of Pain,
The powerless poet who curses his genius.

Shifty, with closed eyes, I feel it watching me
With the intensity of an appalling remorse --
My empty soul. Where to flee? And what haggard night
Throws, fragments, throws scorn on this distressing contempt?

Fogs, arise! Pour your monotonous ashes
Into long rags of mists in the sky
Which will flood the pale swamp of the autumns
And build a great silent ceiling!

And you, fishing in pools of Lethe and collecting
The mud and the weak reeds coming in to you
Dear Tedium, blocking with an untiring hand
The great blue holes which the birds maliciously made.

Again! Let the sad chimneys smoke without resting
And let a wandering prison of soot
Extinguish by the horror of its black streaks
The sun dying, yellowish, on the horizon!

"The sky died." Towards you, I come near! Give, oh matter,
Forgetfulness of the cruel Ideal and of the Sin
To this martyr who comes to share the litter
Where the happy cattle of men are lying

Because I want, because finally my brain, emptied
Like the jar of rouge lying at the foot of a wall
Has no more art to rig out the sobbing idea
Sorrowfully yawning toward a dark demise…

In vain! The Blue triumphs, and I hear it in
The bells singing. My soul, it becomes a voice
To frighten us more with its nasty victory,
And from the living metal comes a blue angelus!

It rolls through ancient fogs and crosses
Your native agony like a sure sword;
Where to flee in this useless and perverse revolt?
I am haunted. The Blue! The Blue! The Blue! The Blue!

Sea Breeze

The flesh is sad, alas! And I read all the books.
Flee! There flee! I feel that birds are drunk
To be among the unknown foam and the heavens!
Nothing, and no old gardens reflected by eyes
Will remember that this heart in the sea is soaking
Oh nights! Nor clarity deserted my lamp
On the empty white paper that defends
And not the young lady breast-feeding her child.
I shall leave! Steamer rocking your masts,
Weigh the anchor for an exotic nature!
Boredom, saddened by the cruel hopes,
Still believes in the supreme goodbye of handkerchiefs,
And, perhaps, the masts, inviting the storms
Are of those whom a wind tilts on the
Lost wrecks, without masts, without masts, nor fertile islands...
But, oh my heart, hear the song of the sailors!

The flesh is sad, alas! I read all the books.
I want to go over there where the birds are drunk
To wander between the sea and unknown heaven!
Nothing, and not the old garden reflected in my eyes,
Will remember that this heart in the sea is soaking,
Oh nights, nor sterile whiteness under the lamp
From a paper defends me from a sick brain,
And not the young lady breast-feeding her child.
I shall leave! Steamer rocking your masts,
Weigh the anchor for an exotic nature!
Because boredom, defeated by the empty hopes,
Still believes in the supreme goodbye of handkerchiefs,
And would you be those, steamer, in the storms,
That charming Fate reserves for shipwrecks
Lost without masts or board, free islands ...
But, oh my heart, hear the song of the sailors!

sigh

My soul rises towards your forehead, oh calm sister,
Where an autumn dreams, speckled with freckles
And towards the wandering sky of your angelic eye
As in a melancholy garden,
Faithfully a white fountain sighs towards the Blue
-- Towards the fond Blue of pale and pure October
That reflects its infinite languor in the big basins
And, on the dead water where the tawny agony
Of leaves wandering in the wind and digging a cold furrow
Lets the yellow sun drag itself into a long beam

Alms

Take this bag, Beggar! You only stroked it
Senile infant of a miserly tit
In order to drain your knell piece by piece.

Draw from dear metal some sin, bizarre
And vast like us, fists full, we kiss it
Blown there so it twists itself! A rousing brass band.

Church with the incense that all those houses
On the walls when the lullaby of a blue one shed light
The tobacco without speaking murmurs the prayers

And the strong opium shatters the pharmacy!
Dresses and skins, do you want to tear up the satin
And drink in your spit the happy inertia,

To wait for morning in the princely cafes?
The ceilings enriched with nymphs and veils,
We toss a feast to the beggar outside the window.

And when you leave, old god, shivering under your sackcloths,
The dawn is a lake of golden wine
And you swear to have stars in your throat!

Because you didn't add up the brightness of your treasure,
You can be decorated with at least a feather, in compliance
To bring a candle to the saint in whom you still believe

Don't imagine to yourself that I speak of madness.
The land opens up, as of old, to those who die of hunger.
I hate giving more and want you to forget me.

And above all, brother, don't go to buy bread.

Gift of the Poem

I bring you the child of a night in Edom!
Black, with bleeding wing, and pale, featherless
Through the burned glass of herbs and of gold
Through the frosty panes, alas, still dreary
The dawn pounces on the angelic lamp
Palms! And when it displayed this relic
To that father trying out a hostile smile
The blue and barren solitude shuddered
Oh nurse with your daughter and the innocence
Of your cold feet, welcome a horrible birth
And your voice, reminiscent of the viol and clavecin
With your withered finger you will press the breast
From which the woman in oracular whiteness pours
For the lips that the virgin blue air starves

Herodiade

I. Overture
II. Scene
III. Canticle of St. John

I: Old Overture of Herodiade

THE NURSE (Incantation):

Abolished, and its ugly wing in the tears
Of the pond, abolished, which mirrors the alarms
The bare golds cudgeling the carmine space
An aurora has chosen, heraldic plumage,
Our funerary and sacrificial tower:
A heavy tomb which fled, a beautiful bird, a solitary
Whim of dawn in the empty black plumage
Ah! The manor of the deprived and sad country
No splashes! The sad water resigns itself
To being visited no longer by the feather or the swan
Unforgettable: water reflects the abandonment
Of the autumn extinguishing its firebrand in it
Of the swan when amid the pale mausoleums
Or the feather plunging its head, desolate
By the pure diamond of some star but
Earlier, which never sparkled
Crime! Pyre! Ancient dawn! Torment!
A purple sky! Lake of the implicated purple!
And on the rosiness, wide open, this window

The singular room in a frame, things
Of the warring century, gilding worn away
Finds them snow-covered, once colored as of old
And its tapestry, the pearly luster, folds
Uselessly with buried eyes

Of sibyls offering their old fingernails to the Magi
One of them, with a past of songs
On my whitened dress in the ivory, shut
In the sky of birds amid the scattered black money
Seeming like flights departing costumed and phantom
An aroma that carries, oh roses! An aroma
Far from the empty bed that a blown-out candle hides
An aroma of cold golds lurking on the packet
A tuft of flowers perjures the moon
(In the melted wax again the one loses its petals)
Of whom the long regret and the stalks of which
Soak in a single vase in the brightness made languid
An Aurora dragged its wings in tears!

Magical shadow with symbolic charms!
A voice, long evocation of the past:
Is it mine, is it ready, the incantation?
Still in the yellow folds of thought
Dragging, antique, like one praised star
On a vague heap of cooled monstrances
By the old hills and by the stiffened folds
Pierced by the rhythm and pure lace
Of the shroud allowing its beautiful netting
Desperate to mount the old veiled brightness
To rise (oh how far in these calls it hides)
The old veiled brightness of the unusual vermeil
Of the languid voice, void, with no assistance
It will scatter its gold by final glories
It, too, the refrain of verses in response
At the time of agony and of dismal fights
And, strength of the silence and of black darknesses,
Everything also returns in the past of the past
Fateful, defeated, monotonous, tired
Like the water of the ancient ponds accepts
She sings, sometimes incoherently,

Pitiful sign!
                    The bed on the vellum pages
So, useless and so monastic, is not the linen!
Who of dreams by folds no more has the dear book of spells
Nor the sepulchral canopy to the desert iridescence
The scent of hair asleep. Did she have it?
Cold child, to keep her subtle pleasure
In the morning shivering with flowers, its promenades
And when the nasty evening has cut the pomegranates!
The crescent, yes, the only one is in the iron dial
Of the clock, for weights suspending Lucifer
Always hurt, always striking anew hourly
By the water clock to the hidden wept drop
Who, neglected, she wanders, and not on her shadow
An angel accompanying her unspeakable step
He did not know this, the king who paid
For a long time the ancient breast was dried up
Her father does not know this, nor the glacier
Fiercely reflecting its arms of steel
When on a recumbent heap of corpses without coffins
Fragrant of resin, enigmatic, he offers
His trumpets of dark silver to the old fir trees
He will come back one day from the cisalpine countries
Early enough? Because everything is predicted and a bad dream!
To the fingernail which rises among the glassware
According to the memories of trumpets, the old
Sky burns, and changes a finger in an envious candle
And before long its redness of sad twilight
Penetrated the body of receding wax!
Of twilight, no, but of red rising,
Rising in the last day that comes to finish everything
So sadly it struggles, we do not know any more the hour
The rosiness of this prophetic time which weeps
For the child, exiled in her precious heart
Like a swan hiding its eyes in its feathers

As they were put by the old swan in his feathers, bereft
Of his hopes, to see the diamonds chosen
By a dying star, which does not shine any more

II. Scene

The Nurse – Herodiade

THE NURSE:
You live! or do I see here the shadow of a princess?
My lips to your fingers and their rings and ceases
To walk in an age ignored ...

HERODIADE:
                                    Stand back.
The blond torrent of my spotless hair
When he bathes my lonely body, the ice
Of horror, and my hair which the light intertwines,
Are immortal. Oh woman, a kiss would kill me
If beauty were not death ...
                                    By what charm
Led and by what morning forgotten by the prophets
Spilled, on the distant dying, their sad feasts
Do I know it? You saw me, oh nurse of winter
Under the heavy prison of stones and of iron
From which my old lions drag their tawny centuries
To enter, and I walk, mortal, the safe hands
In the desert perfume of his ancient kings
But still, have you seen what my terrors were?
I stop dreaming about the exiles and I lose my leaves
As, near a pond whose fountain welcomes me
The pale lilies that are in me, while to fall for,
To follow the languid debris with a glance
Falling, across my reverie, in silence
The lions, of my dress, push aside the indolence

And watch my feet which would calm the sea
Calm down, you, the shivers of your aged flesh
Come, and my hair imitates the too fierce
Ways which cause your fear of manes
Help me, because you do not desire to see me anymore
Has combed it casually in a mirror

THE NURSE:
Nor else the happy myrrh in its closed bottles
Of the essence stolen from the maturity of roses
Do you want to try the dismal virtue,
My child?

HERODIADE:
              Leave these perfumes here, you do not know
That I hate them, nurse, and do you want me to feel
Their drunkenness flooding my listless head?
I would like my hair, which is not flowers
To spread the forgetfulness of human pain
But of gold, forever, virgin of seasoning
In their cruel flashes of lightning and in the dull pallor
Observing the sterile coolness of the metal
Having reflected, jewels of the native wall
Weapons, vases from my lonely childhood

THE NURSE:
Forgive me! The age erased, queen, your defense
Of my spirit dimming like an old book or black. . .

HERODIADE:
Enough! Hold this mirror before me.
                                        Oh mirror!
Cold water frozen in your frame by boredom
How many times and during the hours, saddened
By the dreams and searching my memories which are

Like the leaves under your ice in a deep hole
I appeared in you like a distant shadow
But, horror! In the evenings, in your severe fountain
I have known my dream, scattered, well known, nakedness
Nurse, am I beautiful?

THE NURSE:

                A star, in truth
But these tresses fall—

HERODIADE:

                  Stop, in your crime
That freezes my blood in its veins and punishes
This gesture, famous impiety. Ah! Tell me
What certain demon throws you into the grim emotion,
This kiss, these fragrances offered, and, shall I say it?
Oh my heart, this hand, still sacrilegious
Because you wanted, I think, to touch me. This is a day
Which will not end without misfortune on the tower
Oh day which Herodiade looks on with horror!

THE NURSE:
Strange time, indeed, in which the sky guards you
You wander, only a shadow and new fury
And seeing in you, premature with terror
But still adorable, as much as an immortal
Oh my child, and awfully nice, and such
That. . .

HERODIADE:

      But were you not going to touch me?

THE NURSE:

                              I would like to be
The one to whom Fate reserves your secrets

HERODIADE:
Oh! Keep silent!

THE NURSE:
                    Will it sometimes come?

HERODIADE:
                                        Pure stars,

Do not listen!

THE NURSE:
                    How, otherwise among dark
Terrors, to dream more merciless still
And like the god who pleads that the treasure
Of your grace should wait! And for whom, devoured
By anguish, do you keep the unknown magnificence
And the vain mystery of your being?

HERODIADE:
                                        For me.

THE NURSE:
Sad flower that only grows and has no other emotion
Than its shadow in the water seen with languor

HERODIADE:
Go, keep your pity as your irony

THE NURSE:
However, explain: oh! no, naïve child
Will decrease, some day, this triumphant disdain. . .

HERODIADE:
But who would touch me, respected by lions?
Besides, I want nothing human, and sculpted

If you see me eyes lost in paradise
That is when I remember I once drank your milk.

THE NURSE:
Dismal victim of the fate it was given!

HERODIADE:
Yes, it is for me, for me, that I flowered, deserted!
You know it, gardens of amethyst, buried
Without end in your learned, dazzled abysses
Unknown golds, keeping your ancient light
Under the dark shadow of a first earth
You, stones where my eyes like pure jewels
Borrow their melodious brightness, and you
Metals that give to my young hair
A fatal splendor and its massive look!
As for you, woman born in malignant centuries,
For the wickedness of sibylline caverns
Who speak about a mortal! According to whom, of calyxes
Of my robes, aroma in the wild delights
Beyond the thrill of my white nakedness
Prophesies that if the warm azure of summer
To him, as if native, the woman unveils herself
I saw in my shivering modesty of star
I die!

    I like the horror of being a virgin and I want to
Live amid the terror in which I do my hair
For the evening, withdrawn in my bed
Inviolate reptile smell in the useless flesh
The cold flicker of your pale clarity
You die for you, you who burn with chastity
White nights of ice and of cruel snow!
And your solitary sister, oh my eternal sister
My dream will rise towards you, this already,

Rare transparency of a heart which it dreamed
I only believe in my monotonous homeland
And everything, around me, lives in idolatry
Of a mirror which is reflected in its quiet frame
Herodiade in the clear view of diamond…
Oh last charm, yes! I feel it, I am alone.

THE NURSE:
Madam, do you thus go to die?

HERODIADE:

                                    No, poor grandmother,
Be quiet and moving away, forgive this hard heart
But before, if you want, close the shutters, the Seraphic
Azure smiles in the deep windows
And I hate, yes I do, the beautiful azure!

                                    Waves delude
And, over there, you know no country
Where the sinister sky has the hated glances
Of Venus which, in the evening, burns in the foliage
I would leave there

                        Lighter yet, childishness
You say, these torches where the wax on fire lights,
Cries among the empty gold some foreign tear
And. . .

THE NURSE:
        Now?

HERODIADE:
            Goodbye.
                        You lie, oh bare flower
Of my lips

I expect something unknown
Or perhaps, ignoring the mystery and your cries
Throw away your supreme and bruised tears
Of a childhood feeling among the reveries
Parting finally its cold gems

III. The Canticle of St. John

The sun which glorifies
Its supernatural stopping place
Immediately comes down again
Incandescent

I feel like the vertebrae
Spreading darkness
All in a thrill
In unison

And my head suddenly appeared
Solitary lookout
In the triumphant swashes
Of this scythe

As a frank break
Rather forces back or slices off
The old disagreement
With the body

Fasting, drunk, that she
If obstinate to follow
In some wild leap
Its pure glance

The Afternoon of a Faun
An eclogue

THE FAUN:
These nymphs, I want to perpetuate them

So bright
Their light crimson, that flutters in the air
Drowsy with dense sleep

Will I love a dream?
My doubt, piles of ancient night, draws to a close
In many a subtle twig, which remained the true
Forest itself, proves, alas, that alone I offered myself
So the ideal fault of roses might triumph.

Consider…

If the women you ramble on about
Represent a wish of your fabulous senses!
Faun, the illusion escapes from blue
And cold eyes, like a weeping spring, the more chaste:
But, while the other sighs, do you say she contrasts
Like the hot day's breeze in your hair
But no, by the calm and tired swoon
Choking the cool morning with heat, if it fights
Do not murmur, source of water, that doesn't shed my flute
In the woods, sprayed with agreements; and the only wind
Outside the two pipes quick to exhale before
He scatters the sound in a dry rain
It is, on the horizon unmoved by a wrinkle
The visible and serene artificial breath
Of inspiration, which returns to the sky

Oh Sicilian edges of a quiet swamp

Of suns which my vanity repeatedly plunders
Tacit under the flowers of sparks, TELL
"How I cut the hollow reeds here, tamed
For my art, when on the grey gold of distant
Greenery offering their vines to the fountains
An animal innocence wavers to rest
And that in the slow preludes where woodwinds are born
That flight of swans, no! Of naiads who run away
Or dive…"
　　　　　Sluggish, everything burns in a tawny hour
Without marking by which art scattered together
Too many hymens desired from he who seeks the tone
Then I shall awaken in the first fervor
The right and the only one, under an antique stream of light,
Lily! And one of you all for innocence.

Other than this sweet nothing disclosed by their lips
The kiss, that while low from traitors gives assurance
My breast, virgin of proof, gives evidence of a mysterious
Bite, due to some majestic tooth
But enough! Arcane, such chosen as for confident
The vast and twin reed which one plays under the blue
Which, diverting to itself the trouble of the cheeks,
Dreams, in a long solo, that we amuse
The beauty of the surroundings by the false
Confusions between it itself and our gullible song
And to make so high as the love that varies,
Vanishes from the common dream of the back
Or the pure flank followed by my closed glance
A sound, vain and monotonous line.

The task is thus, instrument of flight, oh cunning
Syrinx, to blossom again on the lakes where you wait for me
I, proud of my murmuring, I will speak
Of goddesses; and by idolaters' paintings

In their shadows they still remove their belts
So, when I sucked the clarity from grapes
To banish regret rejected by my feint
Laughing, I raise the empty cluster to the summer sky
And, breathing on their luminous skins, eager
For drunkenness, I look through it until the evening

Oh nymphs, let us be filled again with diverse MEMORIES
"My eye, piercing the reeds, darted into each immortal
Neck, that drowned its burning in the wave
With a shout of rage to the forest's sky
And the splendid bath of hair disappears
In the clarity and chills, oh precious stones!
I run up, when to my feet, reaching between it, (bruised
From this slowness tasted this evil to be two)
Some sleepers amid their arms, only dangerous
I delight them, without ceasing to embrace them, and steal
To this bed of roses, hated by the frivolous shade
Losing all their perfume in the sun
Where our frolics exhausted the days just the same"
I adore you, wrath of virgins, oh delight
Fierce naked burden of the sacred which slips
To escape my lips on fire, drinking, like lightning
Quivering! The secret dismay of the flesh
From the feet of the inhuman to the heart of the shy
Which abandons at the same moment an innocence, wet
With crazy tears or vapors, not so sad
"My crime, it is to have, glad to vanquish these
Treacherous fears, divided, the disheveled tuft
Of kisses which the gods kept so well mixed
Because I was hardly able to hide a burning laugh
Under the happy folds of the only one (keeping
By a simple finger, so that its feathered innocence
Colored by the excitement that lights up her sister
The little girl, naïve, does not blush)

That from my arms, undone by waves of death
This prey, forever thankless, frees itself
Mercilessly from the sobs which still intoxicated me
Too bad! Draw me toward the happiness of others
By their braid tied to the horns on my forehead
You know, my passion, that, purple and already ripe
This pomegranate bursts, and bees rustle
And our blood, loving the one who will enter
Flows for the whole swarm of eternal desire
At a time when this wood of gold and of ashes is tinged
A feast is kindled in the extinguished leaves
Etna! It is upon you, visited by Venus
Who places her innocent heels on your lava
When a sad nap thunders or exhausts the flame
I hold onto the queen!

Oh certain punishment…

No, but the vacant soul
Of words and this body weighed down
Lately succumbing to the proud silence of noon
Without more one must needs sleep in the oblivion of blasphemy
Lying on the faded sand and as I like
Opening my mouth to the effective star of wines!

Couple, goodbye; I go to see the shade you have become

The Hair

The hair flight of a flame to the extreme
West desires to deploy all
This raises (I would die a diadem)
Towards the front crowned her former home

But without this or that deep sigh naked
The ignition of fire still inside
Originally it only continues
In the jewel in the eye and truthfully laughs

A nudity heroes tend defames
The one that does not star lights moving finger
Nothing to simplify the woman with glory
Performs by his chief dazzling feat

From rubies sow doubt that the scars
And a joyful and tutelary torch.

Saint

At the window which holds
The old sandalwood, its gilt worn away
From its viol glittering
As it used to with flute or lute

It is the pale saint, spreading open
The old book that unfolds
The streaming Magnificat
As it used to at vespers and compline

At this glass of a monstrance
Touched by the harp of an angel
Formed by his evening flight
For the delicate tip

Of a finger that, without the old sandalwood
Nor the old book, she poises
On the instrument's plumage,
Musician of silence

Toast in Memory
of Théophile Gautier

Oh you, the fatal emblem of our happiness!

Greetings from dementia and the pale libation
Do not believe I offer my empty cup
In the magic hope of the corridor where a golden monster suffers!
Your appearance won't be enough for me:
Because I alone have put you in a place of porphyry.
The rite is for the hands to extinguish the torch
Against the thick iron doors of the tomb:
And one knows it not, badly, chosen for our very
Simple feast to sing the absence of the poet
For this beautiful monument encloses him completely.
Except for the burning glory of the craft,
Till the common and vile hour of ashes
Returns toward the fires of the pure and mortal sun
By the pane which lights an evening proud to fall there!

Magnificent, total and solitary, such
Trembles to escape the false pride of the men
This wild crowd! It announces: we are
The sad opacity of our future spectra.
But the image of grief scattered on blank walls
I disdained the lucid horror of a tear,
When, deaf himself to my sacred verse which did not alarm him
Some one of these passers-by, proud, blind and dumb,
Guest of his vague shroud, transmuted
Into the virgin hero of the posthumous wait.
A vast chasm brought in the gathered haze

By the short-tempered wind of words that he did not speak,
The Void to this man since abolished:
Memories of horizons, is that you, oh you, what is the Earth?
Howl this dream, and voice whose clarity fades,
The space has for a toy the cry, "I do not know!"
The Master, by a profound eye, on his steps
Has calmed the uneasy miracle from paradise
Whose final thrill in his voice alone awakens
The mystery of a name for the Rose and the Lily.
Is there nothing that remains of this fate?   Is there?
Oh all of you, forget a darker creed.
The splendid eternal genius has no shadow.
I, because of your anxious desire, I want to see
Who fainted yesterday, in ideal obligation
That we have to the gardens of this star
Surviving for the honor of quiet disaster
A solemn agitation by the air
Of words, purple, drunk and big clear calyx,
Which, rain and diamond, the translucent glance
Rests on these flowers there that do not fade
Isolates among the hour and the ray of the day!

It is the abode already of our true groves,
Where the pure poet's humble and wide gesture
To forbid the dream, enemy of his charge
So that the morning of his haughty rest
When the ancient death is as for Gautier
To not open his sacred eyes and to keep silent
Appears, about the dependent ornamental path,
The solid tomb where everything that can harm rests,
And the stingy silence and massive night.

Prose for des Esseintes

Hyperbole! from my memory
Triumphantly you know how
To arise today like spells in
An iron-bound book

Because I install, by my science,
The hymn of spiritual hearts
In the work of my patience,
Atlases, herbals, and rites

We took our faces for a walk
(We were two, I say we were)
By many a charming landscape
Oh sister, comparing it to you

The era of authority becomes clouded
When, for no reason, we say
Of this afternoon that our double
Unconsciousness deepens

That its site, soil of a hundred irises,
They know if indeed it ever was,
It does not bear a name which quotes
The gold of the summer trumpet.

Yes, on an island which the air charges
With sight and not with visions
Every flower opened wider
Without us talking about it.

Some, immense, as each
Usually adorned itself
With a lucid outline, a gap,
Which separated it from the gardens.

Glory of the long desire, Ideas
Everything in me was excited to see
The family of fleurs-de-lys
Springing up in this new duty.

But this sensible and soft sister
Did not send her glance farther
Than that smile, and to understand it
I busy myself, my old concern

Oh! Let the Spirit of dispute know,
At this time when we are silent,
When the stem of multiple lilies
Grew too much for our reasons

And not as the shore weeps
When its dreary game dissembles
By wanting the magnitude to happen
Amid my young astonishment

To hear all the sky and the boundless
Map witnessed by my steps,
By the stream itself which meandered
When this country did not exist.

The child abandons her ecstasy
And erudite already by the roads
She says the word: Anastase!
Born for eternal scrolls

Before a tomb she laughs
Through any weather, her ancestor,
To bear this name: Pulcheria!
Hidden by the excessive gladioli.

A F*an (Mrs. Mallarmé's)*

As if a language with
Nothing but a fluttering in heaven
The future poetry frees itself
Of its very dear dwelling

Wing in a whisper the courier
This fan, if it is the one,
The same, behind which
You some mirror has it

Clear (where it'll fall another time
Each speck pursued
A little invisible ash
Only to bring me down again)

Always it appears so
Between your hands without idleness

Another Fan (Miss Mallarmé's)

Oh dreamer, for whom I plunge
Into pure pathless delight
I know how, by a subtle lie
To keep my wing in your hand

A cool twilight breeze
Comes to you with every flutter
Whose captive stroke pushes back
The horizon delicately

Dizziness! Here is that shiver—
Space like a big kiss
Who, born crazy for no one,
Cannot gush or die down

You feel the fierce paradise
Like a buried laugh slipping
From the corner of your mouth
To the bottom of the unanimous fold

The scepter of the pink shores
Stagnant in the golden evenings, this is it,
This white enclosed flight which you put
Against the fire of a bracelet

A F*an*

In order for the ice-cold roses to live
All the same will interrupt
With a white calyx swiftly
Your breath became frost

But what my flapping sets free
The tuft by a profound shock
This frigidity melts
In the laughter of drunken blossoming

To throw the sky into detail
Here like a good fan
You agree, better than a flask

Nobody locking up the emery
But that it loses there or violates it
The aroma Mery emanates

1890

Leaf of an Album

All of a sudden and as if for fun
The girl who wanted to hear,
To turn out to be a little like,
The wood of my various flutes

It seems to me that this attempt,
Tried before a landscape,
Had something good about it when I stopped
To look you in the face

Yes, this empty breath that I
Exhale to its uttermost limit
With my several crippled fingers
Lacks the means to imitate

Your very natural and clear
Child's laughter that charms the air

At times, and without a breath moving it
All the nearly incense-colored outdatedness—
As furtively and visibly I feel
The stone widow unveiled by it fold by fold—

Floats or seems by itself not to prove anything
Except to apply time's antique balm
To the suddenness of our new friendship—
We, age-old, people so happy

Oh dear ones, we met in Bruges, which was never commonplace
It multiplied the dawn over the old canal
With the scattered sails of many a swan

When solemnly that city taught me
Which among her sons another flight had chosen
To quickly spread as well the wing-like spirit

Sonnet ("Lady")

Lady
       Without too much heat but at the same time aflame
The rose that cruel or torn or weary
Even of the white dress of purple it will loosen
To hear the diamond weeping in its flesh

Yes without these crises of dew and quietly
Nor breeze although, with the past stormy sky
Is jealous to bring I don't know which space
In the simple day the very true day of feeling

It does not seem to you, let us say, that every year
The spontaneous grace of which your forehead, reborn
Is enough according to some appearance and for me

As a cool fan in the room wonders
To revive a little agitation as it is here
All our native monotonous friendship

Sonnet ("Oh so dear")

Oh so dear from far and near and white, so
Charmingly you, Mary, as I dream
Of some rare balm drifting from a lie
On no vase of darkened crystal

You knew it, yes! For me here are the years, here are
Always what your dazzling smile continues
The same rose with its lovely summer that plunged
Long ago and will do so in the future

My heart that in the nights sometimes searches to hear
Or of that last word, the tenderest, you are called
Impassioned in the one nothing that sister whispered

Were it not a very great treasure, and a head so small
That you teach me well a whole other sweetness
All spoken into by the only kiss in your hair.

Rondels I *and* II

I
Nothing to the awakening that you had
Considered from some pout
Worse if the laughter shakes
Your sure wing, the pillows

Indifferently slumber
Without fear that a breath admits
Nothing to the awakening that you had
Considered from some pout

All the dreams of wonder
When this beauty thwarts them
In the eye diamonds to be paid
Nothing to the awakening that you had

II
If you want we shall love each other
With your lips without saying it
This rose does interrupt
Only to cry a worse silence

Not only songs launch quick
The sparkling of a smile
If you want we shall love each other
With your lips without saying it

Wordless wordless between the rings
Sylph in imperial purple
A burning kiss tears us apart
To the tip of our outermost wings
If you want we shall love each other

Street Songs

I – The Old Shoe Man

Outside the pitch, nothing to do
The lily is born white, as smell
Simply I prefer it
Such a good mender

It goes of leather to my pair to
Add more that I never
Had, it discourages
A need of bare heels

His hammer which goes astray
Fixed with cheeky nails
On the sole the urge
Still leading elsewhere

He would recreate shoes,
Oh feet! If you wanted it!

II – The Woman Selling Aromatic Herbs

Your blue straw of lavender
Do not believe with this daring
Eyelash that you sell it to me
As the hypocrite has it

On wallpaper the wall
Of places absolute places
For the belly which scoffs at
Returning to the blue feelings

Better between an intrusive
Hair here put it there
That the strand feels wholesome
Zephirine, Pamela

Or leads toward the husband
The beginning of your lice

III – The Road Mender

These pebbles, you grade them flat
And it is, like a troubadour
A cube also of brains
Which I need to open daily

IV – The Seller of Garlic and Onions

The tedium of going visiting
With garlic we take it away
The elegy in the tear hesitates
A bit if I split onions

V – The Worker's Wife

The woman, the child, the soup
Along the way for the quarryman
Complimenting him that it cuts
During the custom of getting married

VI – The Glazier

The pure sun which put back
Too much pure brightness to sort him out
Removes his shirt, dazzled,
On the back of the glazier

VII – The Newsboy

Still, the title doesn't matter
Without himself catching a cold from
A thaw, these earnings whistle a liter
Shouting an early edition

VIII – The Old Clothes Woman

The keen eye out of which you look
Up to their contents
Separates me from my clothes
And like a god I go naked

Note to Whistler

About nothing—like the gusts
That occupy the streets
Subject to the black flight of hats;
But then a dancer emerged

A whirlwind of muslin or
Fury scattered in skimmings
When she raised her knee
The same way we lived

For, apart from him, hackneyed
Spiritual, drunk, motionless
Struck by her tutu,
Without otherwise fretting

Otherwise laughing that could be air
From her skirt to fan Whistler

Little Airs I *and* II

I
Some solitude or other
Without the swan or the dock
Mirrors its obsolescence
Given that I abdicate

Here from the loud boasting
Not to be touched
Whose hand a sky so multicolored
With the gold of sunset

But languorously goes along
Like the white linen taken off
Such a fleeting bird itself plunges
She who exults nearby

Into the wave you become
Your bare jubilation

II
Indomitability owed
As my hope dashes to
Burst there above lost
With fury and silence

Voice foreign to the woods
Or echo followed by zero
The bird as we never heard
Another time in life

The dazed musician
That expires in doubt
If of my breast and not of his
Up sprung the worst sob

Shredded it goes whole
Stay on some path!

Little Air (Warlike)

It goes to me to keep silent about it
That I smell of the foyer
Military trousers
Reddening on my legs

I watch for it, the invasion,
With the virgin wrath
Hardly from the stick
To white gloves of dogfaces

Bare or of obstinate exterior
Not to beat the Teuton
But like another menace
At the end it's what I want

To cut short this stinging nettle
Crazy for the sympathy

Several Sonnets I *("When the Shadow threatened")*

When the Shadow threatened with the fatal law
Such an old Dream, desire and pain of my vertebrae,
Saddened to die under the dismal ceilings
It doubtless bent its wing in me.

Luxury, oh room of ebony where, to seduce a king
The famous festoons twist themselves to death,
You are only a pride lied by the darkness
To the eyes of the monk dazzled by his faith

Yes, I know that in this distant night, the Earth
Throws a big brightness on the bizarre mystery
Under the hideous centuries that darken it less.

The space to itself seems to increase or deny
Rolls in this boredom of the vile lights that witness
What was a star in a festive mood turned genius.

Several Sonnets II *("The virgin, the enduring")*

The virgin, the enduring, and the beautiful now
Will tear us with a blow of a drunken wing
This forgotten hard lake that haunts under the frost
The transparent glacier of flights that did not escape!

A swan once remembers that he is
Magnificent but has no hope of escaping
Not to have sung the region where to live
When of sterile winter the boredom glittered

All his neck will shake this white agony
By the space imposed on the bird who denies it
But not the horror of the ground where the plumage is taken

Phantom whom in this place its pure brightness assigns,
It stands still in the cold dream of contempt
That the Swan dresses in its useless exile.

Several Sonnets III *("fled victoriously")*

The handsome suicide fled victoriously
Firebrand of glory, blood by foam, gold, storm!
Oh laugh if over there crimson gets ready
To but welcome on high like my empty grave

What! Of all this brightness not even the fragment
Lingers, it's midnight, in the shadow which celebrates us,
Except that a presumptuous treasure by heart
Pours its cherished nonchalance without a torch

Yours as always the delight! Yours
Yes only from the fainted sky retains
Little of childish triumph by donning you

With clarity when you put her on the pillows
Like a warrior's helmet of an empress child
Of whom to represent you would fall from roses

Several Sonnets IV *("Its pure fingernails")*

Its pure fingernails on high devoted to their onyx
Anxiety, at midnight, supporting a torchbearer
Many a dream of evensong burned by the Phoenix
That does not collect a cinerary amphora

On the consoles in the vacant lounge, no folded shell
Abolished trinket of sound insignificance
(Because the Master went to draw tears from the Styx
With this the only object of which Nothingness is proud)

But near to the window on the empty north, a dying
Gold, according, perhaps, to the decor
Of unicorns kicking out of the fire against a nymph

She, dead, naked in the looking-glass still
That in forgetfulness enclosed by a frame
In sparkles soon after the septet make themselves seen

Allegorical sonnet about himself
(1868 version)

The approving Night illuminates the onyx
Of her nails in pure crime, torchbearer
Of the Evening abolished by the evensong's Phoenix
Whose ashes aren't in a cinerary amphora

On consoles, in the dark salon, no shell in folds
Unusual vessel of sound insignificance
Because the Master went to draw water from the Styx
With all his objects whose dream is honored

And according to the window to the empty north
Harmful gold incites a brawl for its beautiful surroundings
Made by a god who believes to take a nymph

In the darkness of the mirror, the decor
Of absence, except that in the mirror still
In sparkles the septet make themselves seen

Sonnet
(For your dear dead woman, his friend) November 2, 1877

On the forgotten woods when the dark winter passes
You complain, oh captive hermit of the threshold
That this double grave which will make our pride
Alas! Only the lack of the heavy bouquets burdens itself

Without listening to Midnight which casts its empty numbers
A day before exalts you not to close your eye
Before that, in the arms of the old easy chair
The supreme torch has lit up my Shadow

Who often wants to have the Visit has to
For too many flowers load the stone that my finger
Lifts with the boredom of a spent force

Soul in the home so clear trembling as I sit
To live again I just have to borrow with your lips
The breath of my name murmured for an entire evening

The Tomb of Edgar Poe

Eternity at last made him into himself,
The Poet gave rise to a naked sword
His century appalled at not knowing
Whether death triumphed in this strange voice!

They, like a hydra's vile outburst, once heard the angel
Giving purest meaning to the words of the tribe
Proclaimed on high, drank the spell
In the flood of some black mixture without honor.

From hostile soil and skies, oh grief!
If our idea does not sculpt a bas-relief
To adorn Poe's grave dazzlingly

Calm block fallen out of an obscure disaster,
May this granite at least forever bear the marks
Of black flights of Blasphemy scattered in the future.

The Tomb of Baudelaire

Disclosed by the buried temple some sepulchral
Sewer's mouth drooling sludge and rubies
Abominably, some idol Anubis
All of his snout singed as a wild barking

Or that the recent gas twisted the wick dipper
Wiping one knows it has undergone opprobriums
He lights a haggard immortal pubis the flight
Of which according to the lamppost spends the night away from home

What dried leaves in the nightless cities
A votive may bless it, seat herself
Against the marble in vain to Baudelaire

Under the veil that girds her absent with shivers
That the Shadow a guardian poison
Always to breathe if we die of it.

Tomb
Birthday — January 1897

The black wrathful rock that the north wind rolls
It will not stop nor under pious hands
Touching its resemblance to human ills
As to bless some deadly mold.

Here almost always if the pigeon coos
This intangible mourning oppresses many
Clouds fold the star of the following days
Whose flicker will silverplate the crowd.

Who seeks, wandering the lonesome leap
Sometimes outside our vagabond—
Verlaine? He is hidden among the weeds, Verlaine

No surprise that he naively agrees
The lip without drinking or drying up its breath
A slandered creek, not so deep, death.

Homage ("The silence")

The silence, already gloomy, of a piece of silk
Laid out, in more than one fold, on the furniture
Which a settling of the main pillar must
Hasten with the lack of memory

Our, indeed old, triumphal frolic from a book of spells
Hieroglyphs that thrill the thousands
To spread a familiar shiver from the wing
Bury itself instead in a cabinet

Of the smiling original roar they hated
Between those master clarities flowed
As far as toward a square, born for their pretense

Trumpets, loud, golden, swoon over vellum
The god Richard Wagner radiates a consecration
Unconcealed by the ink itself in sibylline sobs

Homage ("Every dawn")

Every Dawn still dumb
Clenching a dark fist
Against the sky blue bugles
Blown by that deaf one

Has the shepherd with the flask
Joined to the hard-hitting stick
Along his steps yet to come
Much as the free-flowing spring rises

By going forward so you saw
Oh solitary one Puvis
De Chavannes
Never alone

Leading your times drinking
To the nymph without a shroud
Who herself uncovers your Glory

"With the only reason to travel"

With the only reason to travel
Besides a splendid and disordered India
This salute - either the messenger
At the time, the cape your stern doubles

As some low yard
Plunging with the caravel
Foamed still cavorting
A bird of new announcement

Who shouted monotonously
Although the bar does vary
A useless deposit
Overnight, despair and gems

For his song reflected until
Pale smile of Vasco.

"The whole soul summed up"

The whole soul summed up
When we slowly exhale
In several smoke rings
Vanishing in other rings

Testifying that some cigar
Burning skillfully for awhile
What separates the ashes
In such a clear kiss of fire

Thus the chorus of romances
At the lip flies there
Exclude some if you start
The real because vile

The precise meaning too. Rapture
Your vague literature.

"Does every pride of evening smoke"

Does every Pride of evening smoke
A torch in a muffled motion
Even without that immortal puff
Being able to defer its abandonment!

The ancient chamber of the heir
Of many a rich and fallen trophy
Would not even be heated
If he arose by the corridor

Necessary pangs of the days that were
Grip as if with claws
The sepulcher of denial

Under a heavy marble which it isolates
It does not light any other fire
Than the brilliant console

"Suddenly there appeared from the rump and the leap"

Suddenly there appeared from the rump and the leap
Of an ephemeral piece of glassware
Without decorating the bitter evening with flowers
The forgotten neck was interrupted

I indeed believe although two have mouths
Drank, neither his lover nor my mother
Never to the same Chimera
Me, sylph of this cold ceiling!

The pure vase of no beverage
That the inexhaustible widowhood
Is dying but does not consent

Innocently to kiss in the most dismal way!
To nothing expires, announcing
A rose in the darkness

"A lace abolishes itself"

A lace abolishes itself
In the uncertainty of the supreme Game
Not to half-open like a blasphemy
Only eternal absence of bed

That unanimous white conflict
From a garland with the same
Buried against a pallid window
Floats more than it buries

But, in the home of him who dreams it gilds itself
Sadly a lute sleeps
In the hollow void of music

Such as toward some window
According to no belly like that of his,
Filial, we would have been able to be born

"What silk with balms of time"

What silk with balms of time
Where the Chimera exhausts itself
Is worth the twisted and native cloud
Which you stretch out of your mirror?

The holes of contemplative flags
Thrill themselves in our avenue
For myself, I have your undressed hair
To bury my satisfied eyes in

No! The mouth will not be sure
It tastes anything in its bite
If it does, your princely lover

In the considerable tuft of hair
Exhales, like a diamond
The shout of the Glories which he stifles

"To introduce me into your story"

To introduce me into your story
This is as a frightened hero
If his bare heel touched
Some turf of a territory

To the glaciers, threatened,
I do not know the innocent sin
Which you will not have prevented
From laughing loudly over its victory

Say if I am not happy
Thunder and ruby in the hubs
To see in the air which this light pierces

With scattered realms
Like the dying purple wheel
Of my only chariot of the evening

"In the oppressive cloud hid"

In the oppressive cloud hid
The descent of basalt and of lava
In the same slavish echoes
Of a snout without virtue

What sepulchral sinking (you
Know it, foam, but drool there)
Supreme among the other flotsam
Abolishes the undressed mast

Or that which the furious fault
Of some high distress
Vainly opens, the entire abyss

In the hair so white that drags
Tight-fistedly, has drowned
The flank, child of a siren

"My books closed again on the name "Paphos""

My books closed again on the name "Paphos"
It amuses me to be chosen with the only genius
A ruin, blessed by a thousand foams
Under the hyacinth, far off, in its triumphant days

The cold roams with its counterfeit silences
I shall not hoot there, in an empty nowhere
If this very white frolic at ground level denies
At any site the honor of the false landscape

My hunger which doesn't feast on any fruits here
Finds in their lack of learning a savor equal to
That which explodes from flesh, human and aromatic

The foot on any dragon where our love pokes
I think, a long time, perhaps desperately
Of the other, in the burned breast of an ancient amazon

This notebook, except for the insertion of a few rejected pieces instead of as tailpieces on the margins:

> *Salute*
> *Fan (Mrs. Mallarmé's)*
> *Leaf of an Album*
> *Remembering Belgian Friends*
> *Street Songs I and II*
> *Note to Whistler*
> *Little Airs I and II*

and the Sonnets

> *The Tomb of Baudelaire*
> *"In the oppressive cloud hid"*

follows the order, but not the grouping, presented in the facsimile edition made from the manuscript of the author in 1887.

Except for some corrections, introduced at the time of the Academic reprinting, the text remains that of the beautiful subscribed publication which later soared to a higher and higher price, which it was able to attain. Its rarity was decorated with flowers, in the original format, again, of the masterpiece of Rops.

No previous versions are given here as variants.

Many of these poems, or studies aiming at better ones, as one tries out the nib of one's pen before keeping them as part of one's work, were abstracted from their box by the friendly impatience of Reviews looking for their first appearance. The first appearance of projects, as points of reference, is noted because the poems were too rare or too numerous. The author himself is of two minds about this, so he preserves them for the reason that the young man he was indeed wanted to take each one into account and to allow a public to form about him.

Salute: this sonnet was composed when I raised a glass, recently, as I had the honor of presiding at a banquet of the review *La Plume*.

Apparition tempted the musicians, and Monsieurs Bailly and André Rossignol have set it to delicious notes.

The Clown Punished appeared for the first time, although it was already old, in the grand edition of the *Revue Indépendante*.

The Windows, The Flowers, Revival, Anxiety (first called *The One Who Is Quiet*), *"Tired of bitter rest", The Bell Ringer, Summer Sadness, The Blue, Sea Breeze, Sigh, Alms* (entitled *The Beggar*) make up the series which, in this work, is named for their appearance in the first issue of *Parnasse contemporain*.

Hérodiade, here a fragment, which used to have only a dialogue part, will contain besides the Canticle of St. John and its conclusion in a last monologue, a Prelude and Finale which will ultimately be published, and which will finish the poem.

The Afternoon of a Faun appeared in a special edition illustrated by Manet. It was one of the first expensive booklets, perfect, like a bag with candies. It was a little bit oriental with its "Japan felt, title in gold, tied up with pink cords of China and black" and was then issued as a poster; then as an engraving, now out of print.

Toast in Memory comes from the joint collection *Théophile Gautier's Tomb: Master and Shade* to whom the invocation is addressed; his name appears in rhyme right before the end.

Prose for des Esseintes. He might have inserted it, perhaps, along with what we read in *A rebours* by our own J. K. Huysmans.

Leaf of an Album ("All of a sudden and as if for fun") is indiscreetly copied out from the album of the daughter of the Provençal poet Roumanille, my old companion. I had admired her, this child, and she wanted to remember to ask me for some verses, this young lady.

Remembering Belgian Friends. I felt pleasure in sending this sonnet to the visitors' book of the Cercle Excelsior, where I had gone to a conference and met new friends.

Street Songs I and II, comment, with diverse quatrains, on the collection of the *Types of Paris*, seen in the illustrations of the master painter Raffaelli, who inspired them and accepted them.

Note to Whistler, appeared in French, as an illustration in the English newspaper *The Whirlwind*, to which Whistler made princely donations.

Little Airs. Number one inaugurated, in November, 1894, the magnificent publication *L'Épreuve*. Number two appeared first in Monsieur Daudet's album.

The Tomb of Edgar Poe. This poem was involved in the ceremony for the erection of a monument to Poe in Baltimore. It was recited to the monument, a block of basalt which America laid over the light shade of the poet, for the country's safety, in hopes that the shade would never rise up again.

The Tomb of Baudelaire. This was a part of the book having this title, published by subscription with the aim of erecting some statue, or bust, or issuing some commemorative medallion.

Homage, between some, of a French poet, inspired by the admirable *Revue Wagnerienne*, dead before the definitive triumph of the Genius.

So much accuracy testifies, pointlessly maybe, to some respect to future scholars.

PROSE POEMS

A pale sky, to the world that ends in disrepair, perhaps starting with the clouds: the worn-out shreds of purple in the west bleed over a sleeping river on the horizon, submerged by rays and water. Trees are bored, and underneath their bleached foliage (from the dust of time rather than that of roads), the house rises on the canvas of the keeper of things past: many a streetlight waits for the dawn and revives the faces of an unhappy crowd, defeated by the immortal disease and the sin of centuries, of men near their sick accomplices, pregnant with miserable fruit, with which the earth will die. In the uneasy silence of all the begging eyes beneath the sun which, under the water, sinks with the despair of a cry, here's the simple pitch. "Nothing teaches you not to enjoy the show inside, because he is not a painter capable of throwing a sad shadow anymore. I am alive (and preserved through the years by the sovereign, science): a woman of the past. Some madness, original and naïve, a golden ecstasy, I don't know what! By her her hair was named, it bends with the grace of cloth around a face which lights the bloody nakedness of her lips. Instead of the vain garment, she has a body, and her eyes, like rare stones! are not as precious as this glance out of her happy flesh: of the breasts raised as if they were full of eternal milk, pointing toward the sky, with smooth legs that retain the salt of the first sea." Bearing in mind their poor wives, bald, morbid, and full of horror, the husbands crowd together: they also, with curiosity, melancholy, want to watch.

When all will have contemplated the noble creature, a vestige of some time already cursed, some indifferent, because they will not have the strength to understand, but the others saddened, with eyelids wet, looking on with resigned glances, while the poets of those times, feeling their faded eyes light up again, moving toward their lamp, the drunken brain, one moment of a vague glory, haunted by Rhythm and in the oblivion of living in an age in which Beauty survives.

Since Maria left me to go to another star – which one? Orion? Altair? Or you, green Venus? – I have always cherished solitude. What long days I spent alone with my cat. All alone I listen, without a material existence, and my cat is a mystical companion, a spirit. I may thus say that I spent long days alone with my cat, and, alone, with one of the final authors of the Latin decadence; since the white creature is no more, strangely and singularly I liked everything which is summarized in this word – fall. So this year, my favorite season, these are the last days made languid by the summer, immediately preceding the autumn and, during the day, the hour I walk is when the sun rests before fainting, with rays of yellow copper on the grey walls and red copper on the stone floors. Similarly, the literature which my spirit demands as a sensual delight will be the dying poetry of the last moments of Rome, since, however, it breathes not at all of the rejuvenating approach of the Barbarians and does not stutter like the childish Latin of the first Christian proses.

So I read one of these beloved poems (on which the patches of makeup have more charm for me than the rosiness of youth) and plunged a hand into the fur of the pure animal, when a barrel organ sang languidly and melancholily under my window. It played in the great row of poplars whose leaves seem bleak even in spring, since Maria passed there with candles, one last time. The instrument of the sad, yes, really: the piano sparkles, the violin gives the light to torn fibers, but the barrel organ, in the twilight of memory, made me dream desperately. Now it murmured a joyously vulgar air and it placed joy into the heart of the suburbs, an outmoded air, commonplace: how is it that its refrain could go to my soul and make me cry like a romantic ballad? I savored it slowly and I did not throw a penny through the window for fear of disturbing myself and realizing that the instrument did not sing alone.

This clock from Saxony, which delays and rings thirteen hours among its flowers and its gods, to whom did it belong? I think it came from Saxony by a long stagecoach in the old days.

(Singular shadows hang on the worn windows)

And your Venetian mirror, deep as a cold fountain, in a bank of gargoyles with their gilding worn away, who was reflected there? Ah! I am sure that more than a woman bathed the sin of her beauty in this water; and maybe, I would see a naked ghost if I looked for a long time.

--Naughty boy, you often say miserable things.

(I see cobwebs at the top of the big casements)

Our chest still is very old: contemplate as this firelight reddens its sad wood; the quilted curtains show their age, and the armchairs' tapestry has lost its make-up, and the ancient engravings on the walls, and all our old fashioned things? Does it not seem to you, even, that the tigers and the blue bird discolor over time?

(Do not think of the cobwebs which tremble at the top of the big casements)

You love all this and that's why I can live with you. Did you not wish, my sister in the eyes of long ago, that in one of my poems these words "the grace of faded things" might appear? New objects displease you; to you too, they are frightening with their garish impudence, and you would feel the need to wear them out, which is very difficult for those who have no taste for action to do.

Come, close your old German almanac, which you read attentively, although it appeared more than a hundred years ago and the kings whom it mentions are all dead, and, on the classic carpet your head rests between your charitable knees on your faded dress, oh calm child, I shall talk to you for hours; there are no more fields and the streets are empty, I shall talk to you about our furniture. . .You are distracted?

(These cobwebs shiver at the top of the big casements)

The Demon of Analogy

The unknown words sang on your lips, cursed fragments of an absurd sentence.

I left my apartment with the clean feeling of a wing sliding on the strings of an instrument, drawling and light, which replaced a voice saying the words in a lowering tone: "The next to last is dead", so that

The next to last
                        Finished the verse and
Is dead.

loosened itself from the fateful suspension in meaning's space more pointlessly. My footsteps echoed in the street and I recognized in the stillness the tensed string of the musical instrument, which had been forgotten, and which the glorious Remembrance certainly came to visit from his wing or from a palm, and, with my finger on the subtlety of the mystery, I smiled and implored from intellectual wishes a different speculation. The sentence returned, virtual, detached from the preceding fall of a feather or of a twig, from then on the voice was heard, until finally it spoke, living from his personality alone. I went (satisfying myself with no more than a perception) reading it as the end of a verse, and, once, I attempted to adapt it in my own voice; soon I pronounced it with a moment of silence after "The next to last" in which I found a painful enjoyment: "The next to last", then the string of the instrument, tense in the oblivion of stillness, doubtless broke and I added as if in prayer: "died." I did not stop trying to return to thoughts of things I favored, soothingly, to calm myself, saying that certainly "the next to last" is the term in the lexicon which means the next to last syllable of a word, and by its appearance, the rest was badly foresworn by a labor of language in which the daily sobs interrupted my noble poetic faculty, the sound itself did so, and the air of a lie arising in haste from my easy assertion which became a cause of anguish. Harassed, I resolved to let the words of sad nature wander in my mouth themselves, and I went whispering with the susceptible intonation of condolence: "The next to last died, it died, it's dead and buried, the desperate next to last" believing thereby to satisfy my unease, and not without the secret hope of overcoming the ever-louder voice when, to my horror! – from an easily perceivable and nervous magic -- I saw my hand reflected in a shop window making the gesture of a caress which falls on something, and I heard the same voice (the first voice, which was undoubtedly unique).

But where the irrefutable intervention of the supernatural settled down, and the fear under which my former spirit was dying began, Lord, it is when I saw, raising my eyes, in the street of the antique dealers that I instinctively made my way down, I found myself in front of the shop of a violin-maker, a salesman of old instruments. Hanging on the wall and on the ground were the yellow palms and wings buried in the shadow, the ancient birds. I ran away, bizarrely, a person likely condemned to carry the grief of the inexplicable next to last.

Poor Pale Kid

Poor pale kid, why shout your pointed and insolent song at the top of your lungs in the streets, until it gets lost among the cats, lords of the roofs? Because that song won't pass through the shutters on the first floor, behind which you are unaware of heavy silk curtains, incarnadine. Inevitably you sing with the assurance of a tenacious little man who goes his own way in life and counts on nobody, working for himself. Have you ever been an era? You don't even have an old woman to beat you and make you forget your hunger when you return penniless.

But you work for yourself, prematurely underweight, dressed in discolored clothes made for a man and too big for your age, you sing to eat, doggedly, without lowering your wicked eyes to the other kids playing on the pavement.

And your lament is so high, as high as your bare head, which rises into the air as your voice rises, and seems to want to leave your small shoulders. Little man, who knows if it will not go away one day, when after having shouted for a long time in cities, you will have committed a crime? A crime is not very hard to commit, it goes, it is enough to have courage after desire, and like that – your little figure is energetic.

No penny falls into the wicker basket your long hand holds, hung without hope over your pants. We will make you bad and one day you will commit a crime.

Your head always raises itself up and wants to leave you, as if it knew, in advance, while you sing with an air that becomes threatening.

It will say goodbye to you, when you will pay for me, for those who cost less than me. You probably came into the world towards that and you go without food from now on. We will see you in the papers.

Oh! Poor little head!

The Pipe

Yesterday, I found my pipe while dreaming a long evening of work, of beautiful winter work. Discarded cigarettes with all the childhood joys of a summer that has passed which illuminates the blue leaves of sun, the muslins, and my grave pipe begun again by a serious man who wants to smoke for a long time without moving, to work better: but I didn't expect the surprise which prepared this relinquishment, barely had I got the first puff, I forgot the big books I had to write, amazed, moved, I breathed in last winter which returned. I had not touched the faithful friend since my return to France, and all London appeared, London as I experienced in its entirety myself only one year ago. At first the dear fogs wrap up our brains and have, over there, a smell to them, when they penetrate under the casement. My tobacco smelled of a dark room with leather furniture sprinkled with coal dust on which the thin black cat rolled around, the great lights! and the maid with her red arms putting the coal in the iron grate, and the noise of those coals falling from the steel bucket, in the morning - while the mailman knocked, solemnly, twice, which made me live! I saw again through the windows the sick trees in the deserted public garden —I saw the open sea often through that winter, shivering on the deck of the steamer in wet mist, darkened by smoke, with my poor wandering beloved in traveling clothes, a long dun-colored dress, the color of the dirt roads, a wet coat which stuck to her shoulders, one of those straw hats without feathers, and almost without ribbons, that the rich ladies discard on arrival, since they are shredded by the sea air, but which the well-loved poor reline for many seasons to come. Around her neck the terrible handkerchief wound, which we shake, when we bid goodbye forever.

How far our civilization is from offering the pleasures attributable to its state! We have to wonder, for example, that an association between the dreamers living in any big city doesn't exist to support a newspaper which notices the hidden everyday events specific to dreams. In artifice as in reality, a good way to fix the mind is between the mirage of a fact, but it rests even on some universal agreement: see, then if it does not, ideally, bear a necessary aspect, clear, simple, it will serve as a type. I, for myself, wrote as it caught my poet's eye, such an Anecdote, before disclosure to the crowd of reporters prepared to assign to each thing its common nature.

The small theater of EXTRAVAGANCES assists at the exhibition of the living cousin of Atta Troll or Martin's classic fairy tale, the Beast and the Genie, and I had to recognize that the invitation of the double ticket yesterday misled me, I put my hat in the vacant stall next to me, my friends' absence testified to the general taste to avoid this innocent entertainment. What was happening to me? Nothing, except: that evasive paleness of muslin taking refuge on twenty pedestals with architecture of Baghdad, brought out a smile and opened its arms to the sad heaviness of the bear, whereas the hero, of these evocative sylphs and their keeper, a clown, in his high nudity of money, mocked the animal with our superiority. Enjoy, like the crowd, the myth included in any banality, and what a relief, without neighbors reflecting on it all, to see the ordinary and splendid day at the footlights found in my drowsy research of imagination or symbols. A stranger to many a reminiscence of such evenings, happenstance seems new! aroused my attention: one of many bursts of applause awarded by the enthusiasm shown on the stage of the genuine privilege of Man came, shattered by what? It stopped clearly with one fixed crash at the height of glory, unable to spread. It was necessary for all eyes to be all ears. The gesture of the puppet, a palm clenched in the air and opened five fingers, I realized that he had ingeniously captured the sympathies of appearance to catch the flight of something in a figure (and all) the ease by which each is taken, an idea that moved in the slight wind, the bear rhythmically and gently lifted, questioned this feat: a claw placed on the ribbons of the human shoulder. A person wasn't panting, though this situation had serious consequences for the honor of the race, what was going to happen? The other leg fell, against an arm along the shirt; and the audience saw a couple united in a secret link, as an inferior man, stocky, good, up on the space of two hairy legs, embrace it to teach the practices of the genius and the skull to the black snout who had not attained half the bust of his brilliant and supernatural brother: but who, him! heightened the crazy mouth of waves, a hideous leader moving by a visible thread in the horror the real denials of a fly of paper and gold. A clear entertainment, more than the vast trestles, with this gift, proper to matters of art, to last for a long time: To perfect it I permitted there to spring a silently forbidden speech from the scion of Arctic sites: without being offended by the probably fatal attitude taken by the mime repository of our pride "Be good (this was the direction), and rather than fail in charity, explain to me the virtue of this atmosphere of beauty, dust and voice, where you taught me to move. My urgent query is just, that you do not seem, in a fear which is only feigned, to answer not to know hurt in the regions of wisdom, the subtle elder! to me, to make you free, still dressed to stay informed of the caves where I dove back in the nighttime humbly, my latent strength. We authenticate by this close embrace, before the multitude sitting to this end, the pact of our reconciliation." The absence of any solid blows to space, in which place I, absolute, was living one of the tragedies of astral history chosen to be performed there, in this small theater! The crowd faded, completely, all in the emblem of its spiritual situation glorifying the scene: a modern provider of ecstasy, alone, with the impartiality of something elemental, the gas, in the high corners of the room, continued a bright noise of expectation.

The charm broke: it was when a piece of flesh, naked, brutal, crossed my vision directed by the interval of the decor, ahead of a few moments on the result, mysterious usually after these performances. A rag substituted for bleeding from the bear, who found its instincts again in a higher curiosity which endowed it with a theatrical brilliance, fell on all fours and, carried the Silence among them all, went walking, suffocated the species, sniffed, and applied the teeth, to this prey. A sigh, almost free of disappointment, inexplicably relieved the meeting: including opera glasses, in rows, attempted, turning the sharpness of their lenses, the game's splendid fool evaporated in fear; but saw an abject meal might be preferred by the animal to the same thing he would have had to first get our image, to taste it. The curtain, hesitating up to then to increase the danger or the emotion, came down suddenly, displaying its newspaper of price lists and common places. I got up like everyone else, to take a breath outside, surprised not to have felt, again, the same kind of feeling that my companions had, but serene because my way of seeing, after all, had been higher, and even true.

Reminiscence

An orphan, I wandered in black and the vacant eye of the family in a staggered row displayed the festival tents, examined the future and what I would be, I loved the smell of the tramps, I forgot my companions around them. No shout of choruses, tears or tirades below, the drama required the holy hour of oil lamps, I wanted to talk to a kid too shaky to be counted among his race, in his nightcap he cut a figure like Dante's companion, who returned to himself, the appearance of a slice of soft cheese, already the essential snow of peaks, the lily or the other whiteness of wings inside, I should have asked him to admit me to his superior meals, shared quickly with some elder, sprung against a canvas near train feats and compatible banalities of the day. Nude, spinning in his quickness, surprising nimbleness to me, him, who also began: "Your parents? I have none. Well, if you knew this farce, a father…even the other day avoided the soup, he made faces just as beautiful, as when the teacher threw the slaps and kicks. My dear!" And triumphed by raising his leg to me with glorious ease. "He amazes us, Dad" then bites into the chaste delight of the very young. "Your mom, you haven't, maybe, you're alone? Mine eats fiber and the world beats hands. You know nothing, parents are funny people who make us laugh." The parade was excited, he went. I sighed, disappointed suddenly not to have any parents.

Stillness! It is certain that on my side, as in dreams, lying in a rocking stroll under the sleep inducing wheels, the interjection of flowers, every woman, and I know someone who sees it clearly, frees me from the effort of uttering a word: the high compliment of examining each costume almost offers itself to the man in whose favor the afternoon ends, who is unable to resist each chance meeting, and this suggests the distant look on his features concludes with a dimple of a spiritual smile. That's nothing, agrees reality, because it had been relentlessly excluded from the rays that expired luxuriously on the shining surface of the landau, like an outcry, amid tacit bliss too, for the dusk of a day in the suburbs, with a thunderstorm, perceived by all the senses at once and for no reason, of laughter (ordinary trident of things and of their triumphal copperwork) in fact, the cacophony that anyone can hear, drawn aside for a moment, rather than what it deserves, from its idea, remaining alive before the dread of existence. "The festival of" I don't know what suburban rendezvous! named the child I transported in my distraction, the clear voice with no weariness: I obey and stop there.

Without recompense for this jolt which needed a plausible figurative explanation for my spirits, as symmetrically arranged by the lantern glass which little by little lit up garlands and attributes, I decided, having missed out on solitude, to sink into myself courageously in the express and hateful fury of all that I had but lately fled in gracious company: ready and not seeming surprised at this change in our program, of ingenuous arms which rest on mine, while we go walking, our eyes on the row, the path of bewilderment that forks in an echo of the same fair's uproar and makes it possible for the crowd to contain the whole universe there for awhile. Subsequently with the onslaught of mediocre licentiousness so as whatever it is that diverts our stagnation, amused by the twilight, at bottom, strange and purple, kept us equal with the naked incendiary, a human spectacle, poignant: denied by the daubed frame or the inscription in capitals on a shack, apparently empty.

To whoever unraveled this mattress to improvise here, like the veils in all eras and the temples, the mystery! belonged, its attendance during the fast, didn't have, with the possessor excited before he unrolled the banner of hope in jubilation, the hallucination of a miracle to show (the futility of his starving nightmare) and yet moved by his brotherly character to make an exception to the daily misery of that field, when the mysterious word establishes the festival, contains the many shoes that trample there (because it peeps into the depths of a single hint of clothing to find one's last cent, his sole purpose to spend it before leaving), him too!, except stripped of any notion that it was necessary to be one of the chosen ones, if not to sell, then to show, but what, had yielded to the call of a kindly meeting. Or, quite prosaically, perhaps the rat, unless educated himself, the beggar counted on the athletic vigor of his muscles, to decide that popular enthusiasm was lacking at that very moment, as is often clear when a man notices the general circumstances.

"Beat the box!" proposed her highness Madame…only you know Who, marking an old fashioned drum which she lifted, her arms uncrossed to signify uselessly the approach of his act with no prestige, an old one of this friendship with an instrument of rumor and of appeal, possibly, attracted to his vacant design, as if it, of all that there had been here, was considered the most beautiful, the mystery, by a enclasped jewel the socialite sparkled, as did her throat, without responding! It rushed, silent clown, to my surprise, to a public halted, grasping the awakening of ruffle and trusted initially deafening the invariable and obscure for myself. "Enter, everyone, it is only one penny, it will be returned to anyone who is not satisfied with the show. " The nimbus doormat in senile palms together thanks gutted I waved the colors as a signal from afar, and my hair, ready to split up the mass in the secret of what had been known to do with this place dreamless the initiative of a contemporary of our evenings.

At the knee, it emerged on a table, a hundred heads.

Clear in one stray shot on the other side it darted electrically, for me, following the fashion, this calculation bursts in the absence of all, a whim or a mood of the sky fully detailed its beauty, without supplement of dance or of song, for the mob paid the alms required, ordinarily favored, and in the same respect I understand my duty in the danger of subtle exhibition, to put aside the desertion in the curiosities and to resort to some absolute power, like Metaphor. Quickly, to blather on until the explanation, on many faces, of their security which, seizing quite as a result, faces the evidence, even with difficulty, implied in the word and agree to exchange its balk against superior and exact assumptions, in short, the certainty for each one not to be redone.

A glance at the last one, with hair that steams then enlightens the splendors of gardens the fading of the hat in crepe of the same tone as the statuary dress being raised, advances to the spectator, on a foot as the rest of the hydrangea.

Then:

The hair flight of a flame to the extreme

West desires to deploy all

This raises (I would die a diadem)

Towards the front crowned her former home

But without this or that deep sigh naked

The ignition of fire still inside

Originally it only continues

In the jewel in the eye and truthfully laughs

A nudity heroes tend defames

The one that does not star lights moving finger

Nothing to simplify the woman with glory

Performs by his chief dazzling feat

From rubies sow doubt that the scars

And a joyful and tutelary torch.

Assisting the living allegory by the waist, in order to hasten her touchdown nicely to earth, she had already abandoned her post, perhaps because my future lacked fluency, "I will remark to you", added I, maintaining the same level with the understanding of the visitors, cutting short their amazement in front of this leave by affecting to return to the authenticity of the spectacle, "ladies and gentlemen, that the person who had the honor to subject herself to your judgment, does not require you to communicate the direction of her charm, a costume or none of the usual accessories of the theatre. This naturally adapts to the perfect reference which the dress always provides as one of the paramount reasons for the woman, and is enough, as your sympathetic approval convinces me." A suspension of appreciative remarks followed, except for a confusing "Of course!" or "It is that!" and "Yes" from the throats as several responded with cheers and with pairs of generous hands, led to the exit over one clearing among the trees and into the night the crowd with whom we were going to mix, were it not for the recruit, waiting in white gloves, childishly murmuring of his dream of flexing them by their estimate of a haughty garter.

"Thank you," the dear one agreed, a puff along with it like a constellation or drunken leaves as if to pierce the calmness otherwise; she had not doubted her success, or at least the ice-cold practice of her voice: I have in mind the remembrance of things that are never forgotten.

Oh! nothing but a commonplace aesthetic...

What wouldn't you perhaps have introduced, who knows? my friend, the pretext to express it in front of me with the related isolation for example of our landau - where is it — let's return there: - but this spouts out, forced, under the brutal punch to the stomach caused by the impatience of people to whom no matter what and suddenly it is necessary to proclaim something, was this the daydream…

Who is unaware of and throws around stripped of fear, across the public; it is true. As you, Madame, would have heard it so irrefutably, in spite of the reduplication of a rhyme in the final line, my patter following a primitive form of the sonnet, I bet if each term had been echoed your way by various eardrums, and would have charmed a mind open to multiple understandings.

Maybe! We should have accepted our thought in the playfulness of the same breath of night.

I rowed a good deal, in a grand, neat and drowsy gesture, my eyes fixed mostly on the inside, forgetting to move, as the laughter of the hour flowed around. So much immobility reclined, like the brush of an inert noise when sailing as far as half the skiff, I didn't check as I docked, and the steady flashing of initials on the oars were laid bare, which reminded me of my identity in the world.

What happened, where was I?

He had to see clearly into the adventure. I remember my early departure, this July of flame, on the interval between its bright dormant vegetation always from a narrow and distracted creek, in search of blooms on the water and with a purpose of finding the place occupied by the property of the friend of a friend, to whom I had to improvise a hello.

Outside the grassless edge a landscape drew me in more than the other, hunted by its reflection under the wave by the same impartial oar. I had come to fail in some clump of reeds, at the mysterious end of my race, in the middle of the river: which immediately widened into a river grove. It displayed the nonchalance of a pond rippled by hesitation from its origin.

Detailed inspection showed me that this barrier of greenery in a point on the course, masked the single arch of a bridge extended to land here and there by a hedge enclosing the lawns. I realized: simply the park of Madame…, welcome to the stranger. A nice neighborhood, during the season, the nature of a person who has chosen retirement also impenetrable wetland that may not be as agreeable to my taste. Certainly, she had constructed from this crystal her interior mirror, away from the bright indiscretion of this afternoon she came and the icy silver mist of willows soon found the clarity of her look familiar to each leaf.

All I mentioned was purifying.

Bent in the sporting attitude that kept me from curiosity, under the spacious silence of what promised to be a stranger, I smiled at the beginning of an offhand slavery by feminine possibility, that did not mean evil, the straps attaching the shoe of the rower to the boat's wood, as if it were one with the instrument's charms.

"Both any…" I was going to finish. Then an imperceptible noise made me doubt if the resident of the edge haunted my leisure, or beyond hope the basin.

The footsteps ceased, why ?

Subtle secret of feet that come and go, lead the mind which desires the dear shadow hidden in the linen and the lace of a flowing skirt on the ground, as to circumvent the heel to toe, in a flotation, this initiative by what walking opened, at the bottom and the rejected folds in the train, a glimpse, of her double arrow, learned.

She knows a reason, at its home, itself the walker, and is it me? aiming my head too high, for these rods not to surpass and all the mental somnolence where my lucidity is, to question that which was hitherto mysterious.

"In what way do you arrange your features, I feel their precision, Madame, interrupting something installed here, by the rustle of an arrival, yes ! this instinctive charm from below that does not defend against the explorer, most authentically tied, with a diamond buckle, of belts. If a vague concept will suffice: and will not transgress the delight tinged with generality that allows and orders the exclusion of all faces, so the revelation of one (do not consider the point in question proven on the furtive threshold where I reign) chased my trouble, for which it has no use."

My presentation, in which this aquatic marauder is kept, I can try, excused by chance.

Divided, we are all together: I am interfering with her confusing privacy, in this suspense over the water where my dream lingers in indecision, better than a visit, followed by others, who permit it. That speech was idle compared to the one I held never to be heard. It was there before it returned as an intuitive agreement that now one could hear the edge of mahogany on the sand which you had!

The break is measured at the time of my determination.

Advise, oh my dream, what to do?

Summarize with a look of blank absence scattered in solitude and, as we gather, in memory of a site, one of these magical water lilies enclosed therein arose suddenly, enveloping nothing in their hollow whiteness, made of intact dreams, of happiness that will not happen and here I held my breath here in fear of an appearance, starting with: tacitly, flexing gradually without a smooth break in the illusion or that the lapping of the visible bubble of foam wrapped in my flight throws at the feet occurring of the person, the transparent resemblance, of the seduction of my perfect flower.

If, caught by an unusual feeling, it seemed, Meditation or Haughtiness, the Savage, the Gay, too bad for this untold wealth that I will overlook forever! because I performed the maneuver according to the rules: disengaged myself, rounded and tacked along the ripple of a creek, sailing like a noble newborn swan, as it gushed into flight, my imaginary trophy, which swelled to something else as if the exquisite vacancy of self love, the summer, continued, down the paths of her park, any woman, stopping, sometimes for awhile, as near a source to cross, or of some body of water.

Spring can push the organism into some acts, that in other seasons are unknown to it. Many a treatise on natural history is full of descriptions of this phenomenon among animals. It would be of more plausible interest to collect some of the alterations brought on by the climacteric moment in the lives of those individuals dedicated to spirituality! Abandoned badly by winter's irony, I carried away, for myself, a state so unmistakable that it could not be substituted for an absolute or naïve naturalism, able to pursue enjoyment in the identification of several kinds of plants. Nothing in the actual case provides any benefits to the crowd. I stole away to reflect on it, under some shadows that surrounded the city yesterday. Gold was their mystery, almost commonplace as I displayed a perceptible and striking example of some inspirations of spring.

Cheers were heard for a little while, in a little frequented corner of the Bois de Boulogne. Imagine my surprise when I saw dark low agitation, through the thousand spaces through the good shrubs that hid nothing, the net result was -- some loud drumbeats of a tricorn hat come to life -- until I saw, the shoes strengthened by silver buckles, a churchman, away from witnesses, responding to the solicitations of the lawn. Nothing similar served the designs of providence. I didn't want to be equally guilty of being falsely scandalized and tossing a pebble from the road. I brought to my smile the same intelligence, a reddening of the face with both hands covering it, that this poor man would show, if he were without doubt discovered in his solitary exercise. To quickly pass, I had to still my voice, in order to not produce distraction by my presence. I strongly resisted the temptation of looking backward, imagining myself in spirit having this almost diabolical appearance, that continued to strain the renewal of his ribs, to the right, to the left, and to the belly, obtaining a chaste frenzy. Everything, rubbing and throwing his limbs, rolling, sliding, resulted in a satisfaction, and he stopped, forbidden as if he were some tall flower stalk with black calves, this distinctive costume worn with the appearance that is in and of itself his wife. Loneliness, cold silence scattered in the greenery, perceived by some senses more subtle than disturbed. You knew the furious flapping of fabric, as if the night hidden in its folds finally emerged shaken! And the deaf crashes against the ground were those of a rejuvenated skeleton; but the fanatic had to stop for you to contemplate it. Hilariously, that was enough in itself to seek the cause of a pleasure or perhaps a duty, which poorly explained a reversion, on a lawn, to the antics of a seminarian. The influence of a spring breeze sweetly expanded the unchanging texts inscribed in his flesh. He also encouraged this agreeable embarrassment to his sterile thought and became familiar again with a contact with nature, immediate, sharp, violent, positive, denuded of all intellectual curiosity, the general well-being, and candidly, far from the obedience and the constraint of his occupation, the rules, the prohibitions, the censures, he rolled in the bliss of his native simplicity, happier than a donkey. That the goal of his walk, met, whatsoever, right and a stream, pointed but not without shaking his pistils and wiping the juices attached to his person, the hero of my vision returned, unnoticed in the crowd and in the habits of his ministry. I would dream of denying anything, but I have the right not to consider this. My discretion, vis-à-vis these frolics first appeared. It had no recompense, except to fix forever, not as a passing dream would bring it to completion, this image marked with a mysterious seal of modernity, at once both baroque and beautiful.

Glory

Glory! I didn't chase it yesterday, irrefutably, and I took no interest in those called by somebody in that way.

A hundred posters absorbing the days' misunderstood gold, the letter's betrayal, fled, to all the city limits, my eyes even with the horizon, departing by rail, pulling away before spending a moment in silence, in a pride hard to understand, which yielded to an approach to a forest at its time of apotheosis.

If discordant, amid the exaltation of the hour, a shout distorted this name, known to unfold the continuity of the trees' points later to disappear, Fontainebleau, of which I thought, despite the broken window of the compartment, to jam my fist against the throat of the interrupter: Be quiet! Do not disclose the fact of a barking indifferent shadow creeping into my mind here, the car doors flying in an inspired and egalitarian wind, and the omnipresent tourists vomited out. The deceptive tranquility of rich woods suspends some extraordinary state of illusion. How do you answer me? These travelers, they have left the capital to come to your train station, good employee, vociferous in your duty, and for which I expect, far from seizing drunkenness to all apportioned by the joint generosities of nature and of the State, nothing but a prolonged silence, time to isolate myself from the urban delegation toward the ecstatic torpor of the foliage below, too immobilized so that a crisis soon flutters them in the air. Here, without disturbing your integrity, is a coin.

An inadvertent uniform invited me toward some barrier. I hand over, without saying a word, instead of the metal seducer, my ticket.

Obeyed, even so, yes, seeing only the asphalt spread unevenly, because I cannot even imagine that this pompous October, these million lives piling up their emptiness in the monotony of the enormous capital, who will erase here the obsession with the whistle blast under the haze, none of which is going to fade secretly as I felt it, this year, of bitter and bright sobs, many a vague floating idea, leaving the fates as branches, such as shivering and what looks like autumn under the heavens.

Nobody is, the arms of doubt flown away like one who carries also a prize of a secret splendor, too pricelessly magnificent to appear! But without the sudden rush forward in this veiled day of immortal trunks discharging on superhuman arrogance (now, should we not view it for what it is?), nor cross the threshold where torches burn away, under heavy guard, all dreams prior to the purple glow reverberating in the clouds of the universal sacred royal intruder who has only come. I waited, for that being, who slowly started the common movement again, reduced to the proportions of a childish chimera carrying the world somewhere, and the train let me off there alone.

A suggestion emanates from me – if, variously, quoted to praise or blame me—I claim it with those who crowd in here – if a summary is wanted, it is that everything in the world exists to end up in a book.

The qualities demanded for this work, certainly the genius of it, terrify me, one among the lacking: not to end there, admittedly this volume is unsigned. What say you: the anthem, harmony and delight, like a pure set grouped in some lightning happenstance of relations between everything. The man, charged with seeing divinely, on account of the connection, at will, crystal clear, expressed only in the parallelism of the pages, before his gaze.

It brings me joy if the air, in passing, half-opens that kind of a new publication on a park bench, and, at random, appears to give life to the exterior of the book: several pages – from so many sprang the outline – no one since then has read it, perhaps no one has even thought about it. Taking the opportunity to do so, when, freed, I set it aside, the newspaper dominates, 'twas mine, the same, it took wing, near the jealous roses, as it covered their blazing and arrogant consultation, then extended among the flower beds. I left the words, also, flowers to their silence, and suggested one discern technically how this scrap differs from the book, itself supreme. A newspaper remains the point of departure; literature passes itself off there as it pleases.

Yet—

The folding is, in relation to the large printed page, a sort of religious sign, that doesn't strike us so much as the slight subsidence in thickness, offering the tiny tomb, indeed, of the soul.

All that is found at the printing house is summed up under the name of the Press, until now, basically, in the newspaper: the page itself is the same, as it has received the impression showing, in the first instance, crudely, the flow of a text. This use, immediately or just prior to the close of production, certainly brings the writer conveniences, proclamations joined end to end, tests, that yield improvisation. So, strictly, this way "a daily" had a vision, little by little, but whose vision? it appeared to have a meaning, even the charm, I will say, of a working-class spectacle. You follow – the elite, or, the upper crust of Paris, their superior disengagement, across a thousand obstacles, affected indifference, and were thrown down and driven back from the situation, as if by an electric fire, long after the articles appeared, in a series, the original constraint, the advertisement on the fourth page, between an incoherence of inarticulate cries. A spectacular, certainly, a moral one, is perhaps what is missing in the newspaper's exploit, in its attempt to outshine the book, although visibly it is still joined from below or rather to its origins, by its pagination, by the serial that commands the majority of columns, nothing, or almost. If the book delays it becomes like a spillway, indifferent, where the newspaper empties. . . until the size futilely and vainly contributes this extraordinary interference of the folding or the initial rhythm, like a gathered flight ready to widen out, because an unopened page could contain a secret the silence there remains precious and the evocative signs follow because the spirit, to everyone, is literally abolished. Yes, without the refolding of the paper and those underneath, that it settles onto, the scattered shadow in black characters wouldn't have introduced a reason to spread out, like a fragment of mystery, on the surface, in the spreading open, lifted by the finger.

A newspaper, the page spread out fully, borrows the impression, an excessive result of simple blurred printing: no doubt that the brilliant and common advantage would be in the vulgarity of the multiplication of the copies and would lie in the printing. A prime miracle, this kindness, in the best sense, or the words, what they originally amounted to, the job, endowed with an infinite number, until it crowns a language, of some twenty letters, their future, all there, returning later, rising up, its principle – approaching a rite – typographic composition.

The book, the total expansion of the letter, had to print from it, directly, an expressiveness and spaciousness by connections, to institute a game one doesn't know, which confirms the story.

No accident, there, where chance appears to capture the idea, the apparatus is the same, not to judge in consequence, these words – industrial or having the features of materiality: the making of the book, in the collection, which will bloom, starts with, starts from an immemorial phrase, the poet knew the place of that verse, in the sonnet, that was written down for the spirit, or surface, pure space. On my review, I will disregard the volume and a marvel that summons its structure if I am not able to knowingly imagine such a reason in view of a special place, a page and its height, to the outlook of its day or, to the work. More the successive, incessant coming and going of a glance, a line finished, to the following one, to recommence, the same practice doesn't represent the delight having immortally, broken off, an hour, with all, to translate its chimera. Another way or apart from a performance like pieces on a piano, energetic, measured by the pages—what closes one's eyes to dream? This presumption is not tedious subjection but the initiative, whose flash of lightning is at home with whoever links up to the fragmented notation.

A hermit tacitly plans, devotes himself to his reading, to the spirit who wins back the meaning in a fainter tone, no mental means extoll the symphony, not absent, but scarce, and it is everything – on account of thought. Poetry approaches the idea, is music, par excellence, doesn't consent to any inferiority.

Here is, in the actual instance, that for my part, yet, concerning pamphlets to read after the current usage, I brandish a knife like a cook, cutting the throats of poultry.

The virgin refolding of the book, still, invites a sacrifice, which bleeds, the red edge of ancient tomes, the introduction of a weapon, or a paper-knife, to establish the hold of ownership. How personal, more before the consciousness, without this barbaric imitation, when it will develop its contribution to the book, took from here, from there, varied in resemblances, guessed, like a riddle, almost made again by oneself. The folds perpetuate a scar, intact, inviting, to open, to close, the page, in accordance with the master. If blind, and a little, one proceeded, the attack is consumed in the destruction of a fragile inviolability. The sympathy would go to the newspaper, placed, sheltered from this treatment: its influence, nevertheless, is regrettable, taxing to the organism, complex, required by literature, to the divine book — a monotony — always, the unendurable column, that one is satisfied with distributing in dimensions of the page, hundreds and hundreds of times.

But…

I understand it can cease to be there this way, and I go in a gap because the work alone or in preference to, has to, for example, comply with the details of curiosity. Why — a spurt of greatness, of thought, or of agitation, considerable, a phrase pursued, in large letters, one line per page, to a graduated position, he would not keep the reader in breathing for the length of the book, appealing to his power of enthusiasm, with tiny groups of, after their importance, explanatory or derived, a sowing of embellishments.

Affectation, to surprise by articulated, far-off onlookers, I agree, if several people I don't cultivate, noticing, by instinct, came from another place where they set out their writings in a fashion no longer current, decoratively, between the phrase and the verse, certain similar features to this one, yet as it is wanted, isolated or for the good name of clear-sightedness, demanded by the age, where everything appears. That one divulges its intuition theoretically and perhaps well, empty like a date, he knew, of such suggestions which attain the literary art, to which one has to hold oneself closed. The hesitation, all the same, of all to discover, abruptly, what is not still, weaves, by modesty, to the general surprise. Let us attribute to the dreams, before we read, in a flowerbed, the attention which seeks some white butterfly, this one here, at the same time, everywhere and nowhere, it fainted not without something high-pitched and naive, where I reduced the subject, all in a little while it had passed and passed again with insistence, before my astonishment.

POEM

A THROW OF THE DICE NEVER WILL ABOLISH CHANCE

A THROW OF THE DICE

NEVER

EVEN IF THROWN IN

ETERNAL CIRCUMSTANCES

FROM THE DEPTH OF A SHIPWRECK

WHETHER
the

Gulf

whitened
becalmed
furious
under a flat
incline desperately

from a wing

its own

by

advance declined from an evil to lift up the flight
                    and covering the spurts
                               and cutting short the leaps

      completely sum up inside

the shadow buried in the depths by this alternative veil

                   as far as to adapt
                      to the breadth

        its gaping depth as long as the hull

              of a ship

          tilted by one or the other edge

THE MASTER

appeared
deducing

of this upheaval

that

as one threatens

the unique number that can not

hesitates
corpse by the arm
rather
that to play
maniacal, grey with age
the part
in the name of the waves

one

shipwreck that

                    outside of ancient calculations
                where the maneuver, forgotten, with age

                            formerly he grasped the helm

of the unanimous horizon
                                    at his feet
gets it ready
     stirs and mixes
          with the fist which would embrace him
a fate and the winds

be another

                    Mind
                         to throw it
                                 in the storm
                         to re-bend the division and to cross proudly

pushed aside from the secret he holds

invades the leader
 sinks in subdued beard

direct from the man

             without a nave
                     anywhere
                            vain

ancestrally not to open the hand
                              wrinkled
                              beyond the useless head

   legacies in the disappearance

                              of somebody
                                             ambiguous

                 the last, age-old, demon

with
        the nonexistent countries
                                 induces
                 the old man into this supreme conjunction with probability

                                                    that
                                             his childish shadow
caressed and polished and returned and washed
                                   softened by the wave and subtracted
                 from the tough bones lost between the planks

                                             born
                                                  of a frolic
the sea by the tempting ancestor or the ancestor against the sea
                 an idle chance
                                                            Engagement
which
        the veil of illusion spattered their obsession
        as well as the ghost of a gesture

                              will hesitate
                              will collapse

                              madness

WILL ABOLISH

AS IF

An insinuation

in the silence

in some close

acrobatics

simple

   rolled up with irony
                or
                  the hasty
                        mystery
                              screamed

whirlwind of hilarity and of horror

around the abyss
                    without sprinkling
                          or running away

                  and rocking the blank index

                                                        AS IF

solitary feather overcome

except

that the meeting or the touching of a cap at midnight
and immobilizes
by the velvet crumpled by a dark laughter

this rigid whiteness

derisory

in opposition to the sky

too much

not to stand out

narrowly

whoever

prince bitter from the danger

would cap as the heroic
irresistible but content
by his small reason virile

by lightning

anxious

      expiatory and pubescent

                     silent

The lucid and seigniorial plume
    on the invisible forehead
sparkles
    then shadowing
    a dark good-looking stature
    in his twisting of siren

    by the final impatient scales

laughs

that

IF

of dizziness

up

the time
to enkindle
bifurcated

a rock

false mansion
immediately
evaporated in fog

which imposed
an edge to infinity

IT WAS
stemming from stellar

IT WOULD BE
the worst
not
more or less
but equally as much

THE NUMBER

IT EXISTED
otherwise like a sparse hallucination of agony

IT BEGAN AND IT CEASED
rising up that denied and closed when it appeared
finally
by some profusion spread in rarity
IT ADDED UP

clearly the sum for a little

IT ILLUMINATED

CHANCE

Falls
   the feather
      rhythmically suspended from the accident
               to bury itself
          in original foams
not long ago as far as his frenzy leapt to a top
        withered
      by the same neutrality of an abyss

NOTHING

of the memorable crisis
or it was
the event

carried out with the aim of no useless result

                                  human

              WILL HAVE TAKEN PLACE
           a common rise toward the absence

                                THAT THE PLACE
lapping lower as any to disperse the empty act
                         abruptly as otherwise
              by his lie
                  had based
              the perdition

in these parts
            of the wave
                 in which all reality dissolves

EXCEPTING
at the height
PERHAPS
so far as a place

merges with the beyond

                                                except the interest
                        as for him indicated
                                                        generally
to such indirectness by such a slope
                        of lights

                towards
                        it has to be
                        The Seven Stars also North

                                        A CONSTELLATION

                        cold of forgetting and of disuse
                                                not so much
                                        that it enumerates
                                on some vacant and superior surface
                                        the successive clash
                                                        sidereally
                        of a total count in formation

watching over
                doubting
                        rolling
                        glittering and meditating

                                        before it stops itself
                        in some last point which consecrates it

                Every Thought emits a Roll of the Dice

I started to translate Mallarmé's poems because I wasn't content with the English versions I could find. In translation, poets who preceded and followed Mallarmé are accessible to us. Baudelaire is accessible to us, Apollinaire is accessible to us. I couldn't find a way into Mallarmé in the English versions I found, and I suspected it wasn't his fault.

Mallarmé was an English teacher, and he did translations of the poems of his beloved Edgar Allan Poe, in prose, of course. But his poems in French were metrical and rhymed. Sometimes the meaning of his poems is guided, let us say, by the rhyme and meter he chose, "ceding the initiative to words" as he wrote in *Variations sur un sujet*. There are alternate homophonic readings of some of his lines as well, that could never be rendered into another language as poetry, only as notes. My inability to reproduce the multiple layers of Mallarmé's poems in French into American verse is a disappointment, but an inevitable one. Those layers rely on sound similarities that aren't available in our language.

Most translations of Mallarmé into English rhyme and use traditional meters. This seemed to me to be the wrong approach. We have seen how Mallarmé approached translating Poe, after all. Mallarmé translated this way moves even further away from the meaning of the poem as a second rhyme scheme, this time in English, imposes an alien framework over the poem. These translations, no matter how carefully constructed, often sound academic to me.

I come from a poetry tradition that learned a great deal from 20th century French poetry, Apollinaire, Reverdy, Desnos and all the rest of them. Some of the great pleasures in music in 20th century American poetry come from responses to French poetry, for instance, John Ashbery's *The Tennis Court Oath*, or Charles Olson's Rimbaud takeoff *Variations done for Gerald Van Der Wiele*, or Ted Berrigan's translations of French poetry in *Bean Spasms*. Hopefully the music I heard there echoes a little in these versions.

I can recommend a great book on Mallarmé and how he wrote -- Roger Pearson's *Unfolding Mallarmé* (Clarendon Press, 1996). The translations of Mallarmé's poems into English prose by Anthony Hartley (Penguin, 1965) appear to me to be more faithful, on the whole, and read more fluidly, than others I have seen.

The translation of "The book, spiritual instrument" is dedicated to the memory of Allan Kornblum, my friend and publisher.

Made in the USA
Monee, IL
04 September 2021

77394495R00083